GRAPHIC HISTORY

THE BATTLE OF THE

by Matt Doeden
illustrated by Charles Barnett III
and Phil Miller

Consultant:
Sally Koch
Assistant Coordinator of Educational Programs
The Alamo, San Antonio, Texas

Capstone
PRESS

Mankato, Minnesota

Graphic Library is published by Capstone Press,
151 Good Counsel Drive, P.O. Box 669, Mankato, Minnesota 56002.
www.capstonepress.com

Printed in the United States of America

1 2 3 4 5 6 10 09 08 07 06 05

Library of Congress Cataloging-in-Publication Data
Doeden, Matt.
The Battle of the Alamo / by Matt Doeden; illustrated by Charles Barnett, III. and Phil Miller
p. cm.—(Graphic library. Graphic history)
Includes bibliographical references and index.
ISBN 0-7368-3832-5 (hardcover)
ISBN 0-7368-5242-5 (paperback)
1. Alamo (San Antonio, Tex.)—Siege, 1836—Juvenile literature. I. Barnett, Charles, III. and Phil Miller. II. Title. III. Series.
F390.D64 2005
976.4'03—dc22 2004014483

Summary: The story of the 1836 Battle of the Alamo is told in a graphic-novel format.

Editor's note: Direct quotations from primary sources are indicated by a yellow background.

Direct quotations appear on the following pages:
Page 5, from *The Fall of the Alamo*, the personal account of Dr. John Sutherland taken from Texas A&M Digital Library (http://dl/tamu.edu/Projects/sodct/sthland1.htm).
Page 8, letter of William Travis dated February 24, 1836, taken from Texas State Library and Archives Commission (http://www.tsl.state.tx.us/treasures/republic/alamo/travis-about.html).
Page 13, letter of William Travis to David Ayers dated March 3, 1836, provided by Sally Koch, Assistant Coordinator of Educational Programs at the Alamo in San Antonio, Texas.
Page 14, Translation of Santa Anna's formal written orders to troops dated March 5, 1836, from Texas A&M Digital Library (http://dl.tamu.edu/Projects/sodct/dewitt.htm).
Page 17, Account of Travis' slave, Joe, taken from *Duel of Eagles: the Mexican and U.S. fight for the Alamo* by Jeff Long (New York: Morrow, 1990).
Page 27, Sam Houston's speech taken from *Eighteen Minutes: The Battle of San Jacinto and the Texas Independence Campaign* by Stephen L. Moore (Dallas: Republic of Texas Press, 2004).

Credits

Art Directors
Jason Knudson
Heather Kindseth

Storyboard Artist
Keith Wilson

Editor
Heather Adamson

Colorist
Brent Schoonover

Acknowledgments
Capstone Press thanks Philip Charles Crawford, Library Director, Essex High School, Essex, Vermont, and columnist for *Knowledge Quest*, for his assistance in the preparation of this book.

Special thanks to Charles Barnett III and Phil Miller at Cavalier Graphics.

TABLE ★★★ of CONTENTS

CHAPTER 1

SURRENDER OR DIE

In the early 1830s, Texas belonged to Mexico. The Mexican government had invited Anglos from the east to settle Texas. Many Anglos became Texans. They built homes and ranches. Even so, Texans had no say in the Mexican laws they had to follow. The Texans wanted to form their own country. Mexican President General Antonio López de Santa Anna wanted the ideas of freedom out of Texas.

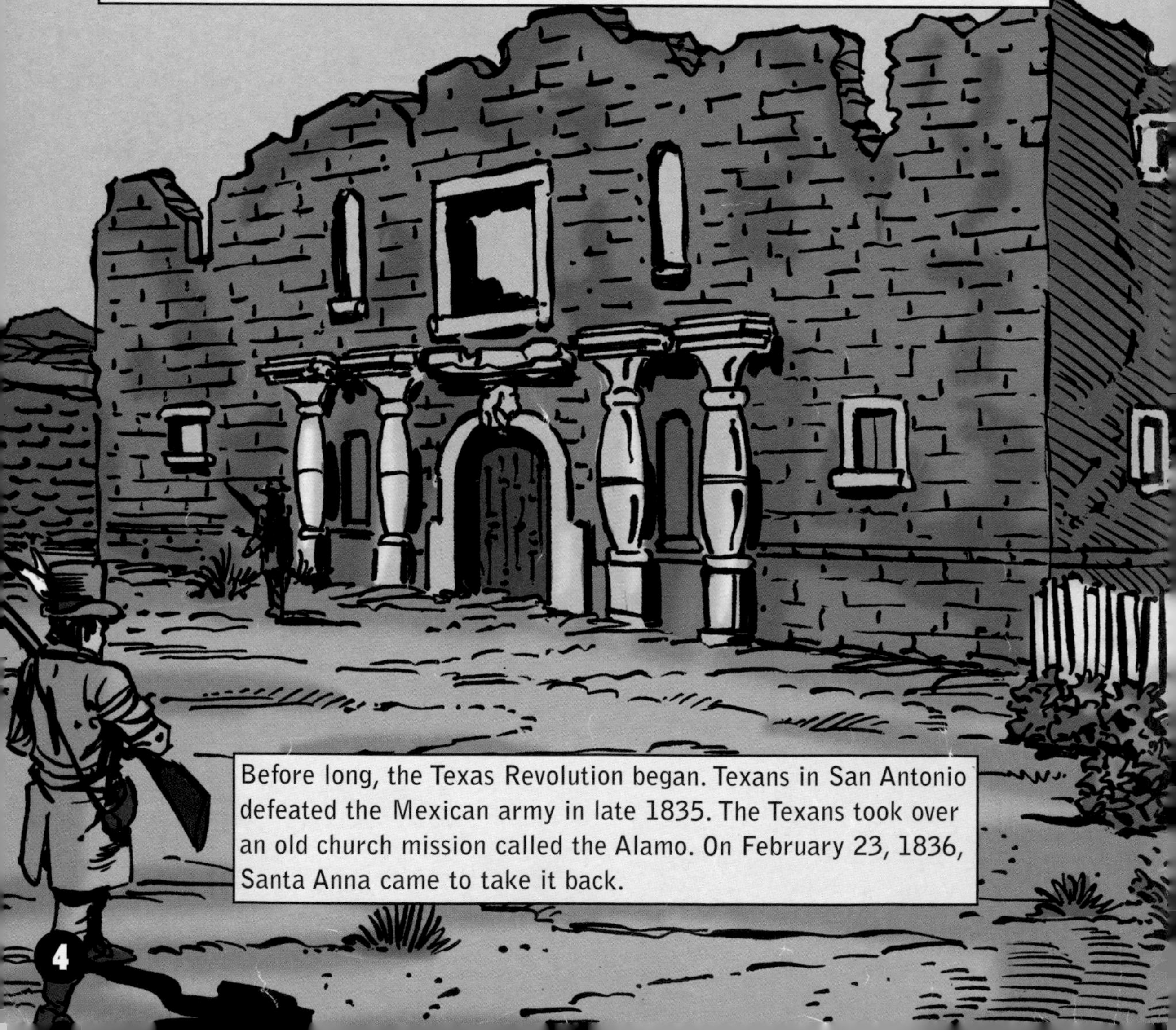
Before long, the Texas Revolution began. Texans in San Antonio defeated the Mexican army in late 1835. The Texans took over an old church mission called the Alamo. On February 23, 1836, Santa Anna came to take it back.

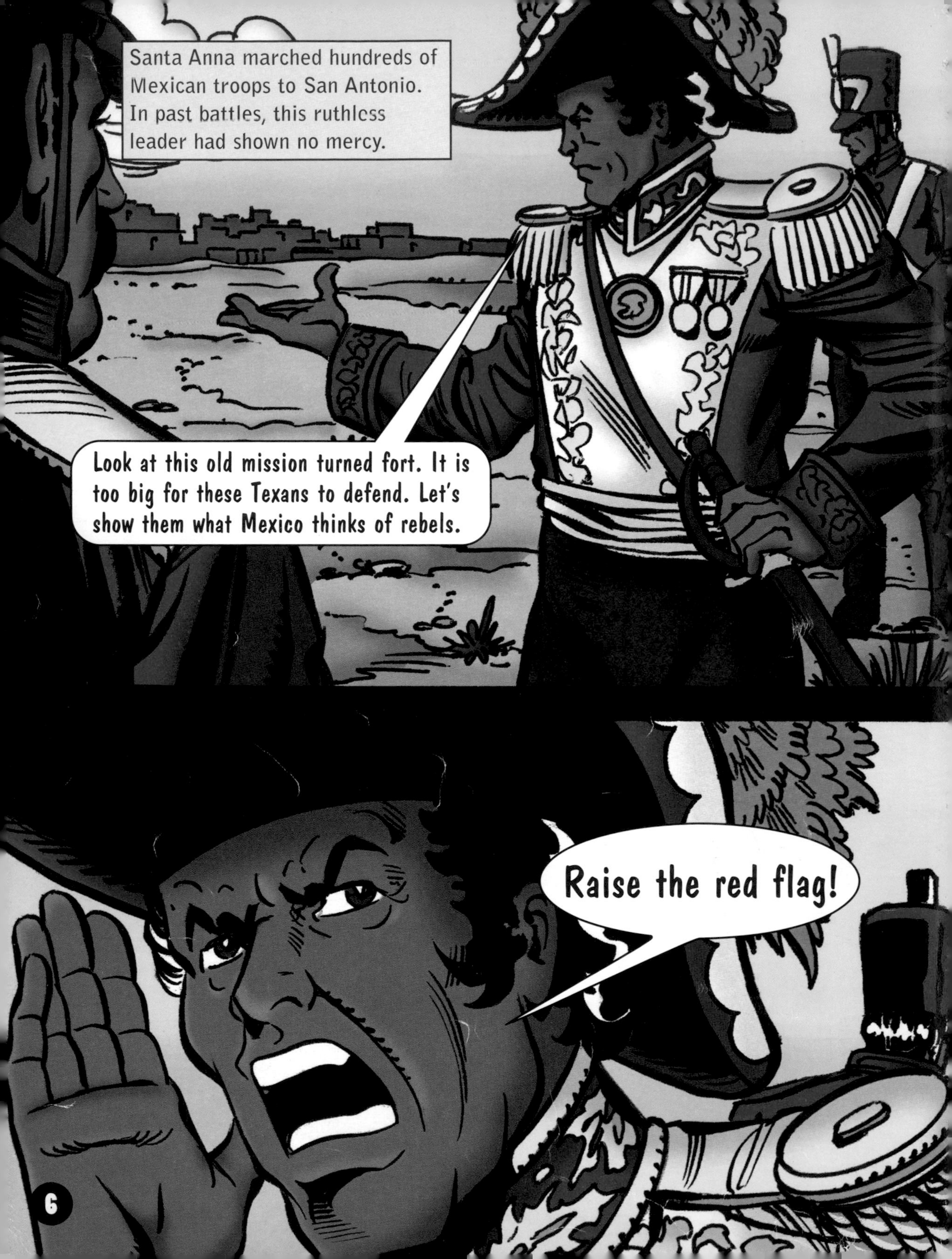
Santa Anna marched hundreds of Mexican troops to San Antonio. In past battles, this ruthless leader had shown no mercy.
Look at this old mission turned fort. It is too big for these Texans to defend. Let's show them what Mexico thinks of rebels.
Raise the red flag!

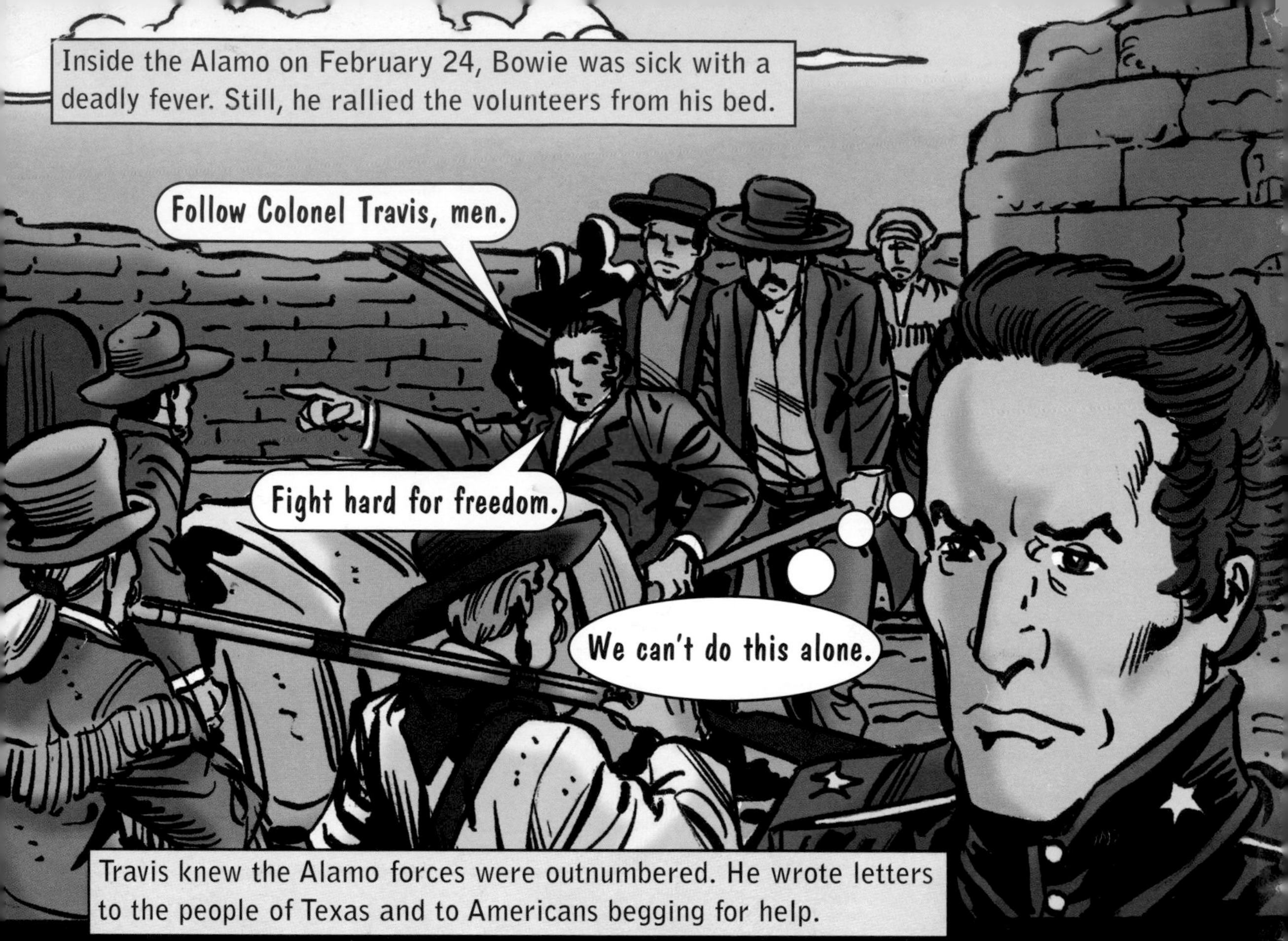
Inside the Alamo on February 24, Bowie was sick with a deadly fever. Still, he rallied the volunteers from his bed.
Follow Colonel Travis, men.
Fight hard for freedom.
We can't do this alone.
Travis knew the Alamo forces were outnumbered. He wrote letters to the people of Texas and to Americans begging for help.

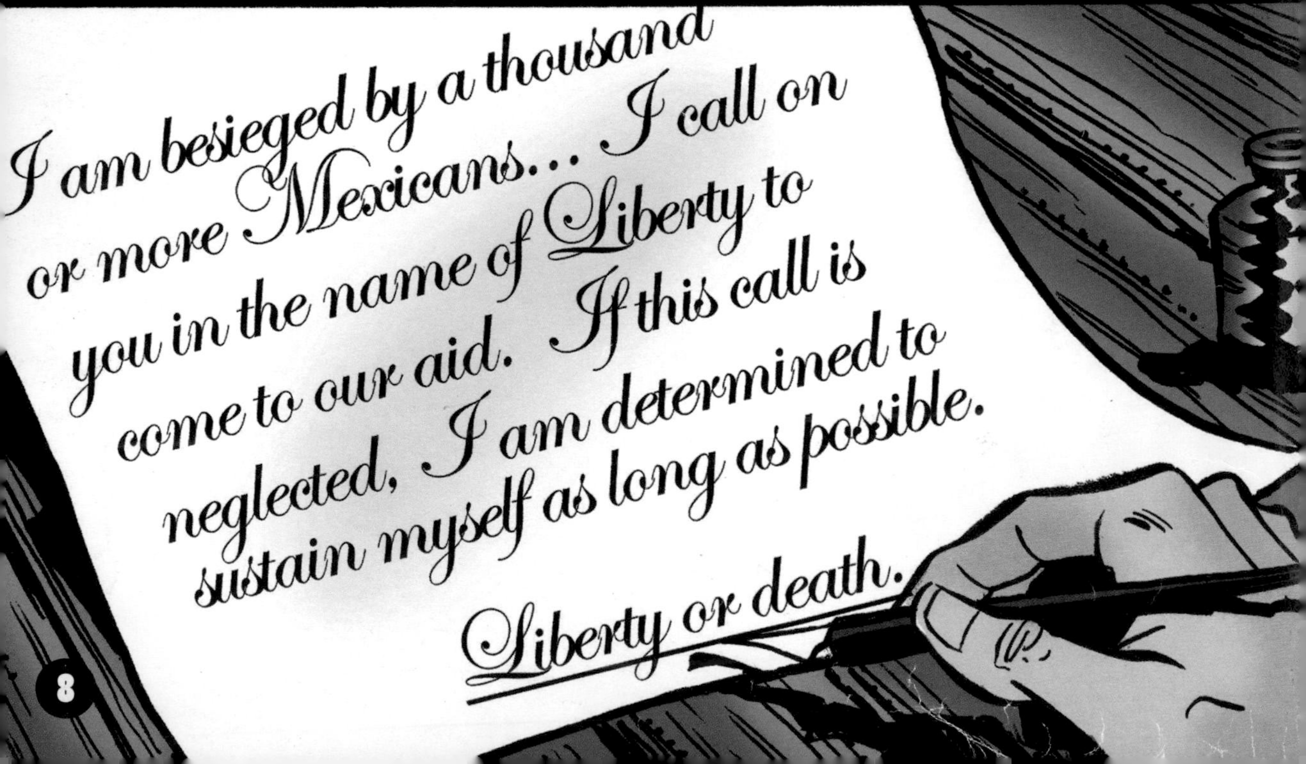
I am besieged by a thousand or more Mexicans... I call on you in the name of Liberty to come to our aid. If this call is neglected, I am determined to sustain myself as long as possible.
Liberty or death.

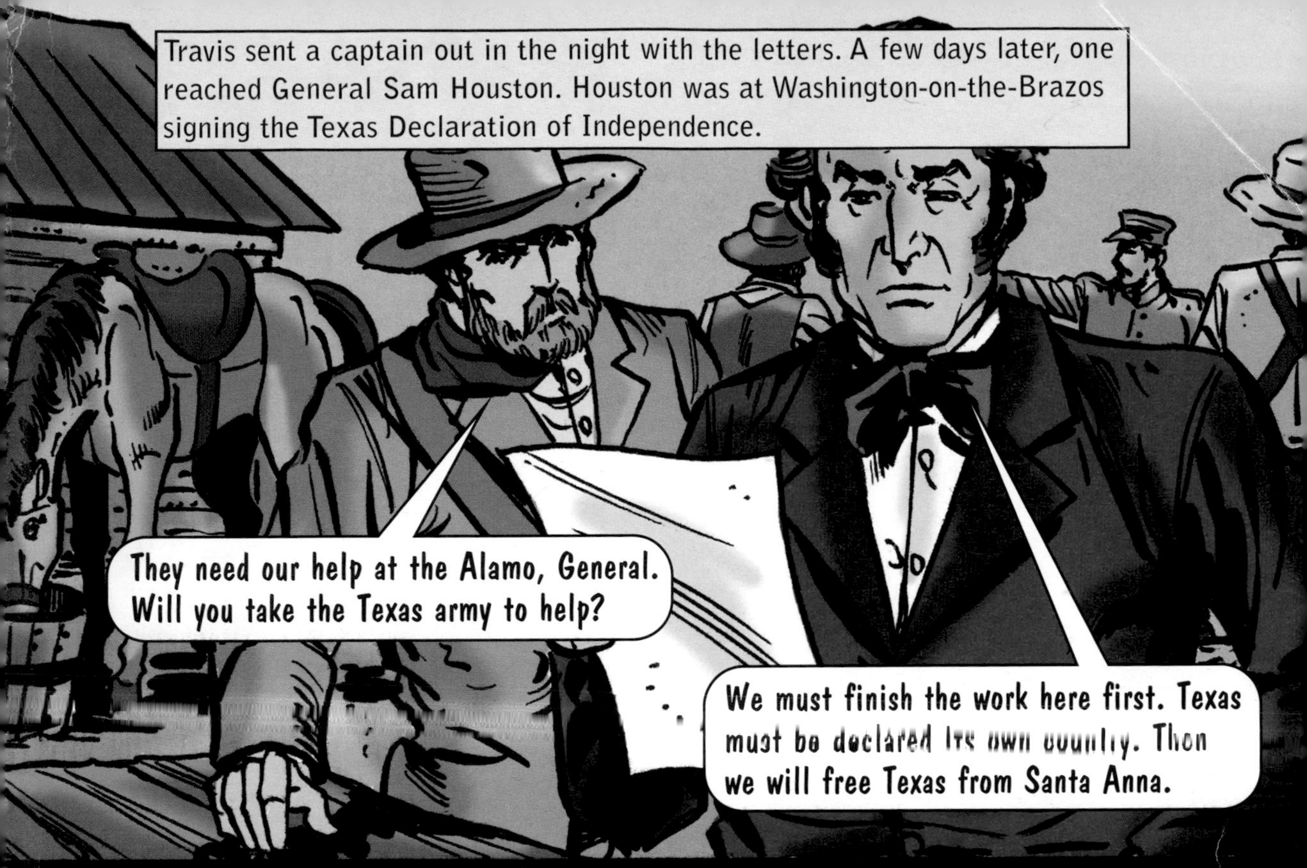
Travis sent a captain out in the night with the letters. A few days later, one reached General Sam Houston. Houston was at Washington-on-the-Brazos signing the Texas Declaration of Independence.
They need our help at the Alamo, General. Will you take the Texas army to help?
We must finish the work here first. Texas must be declared its own country. Then we will free Texas from Santa Anna.

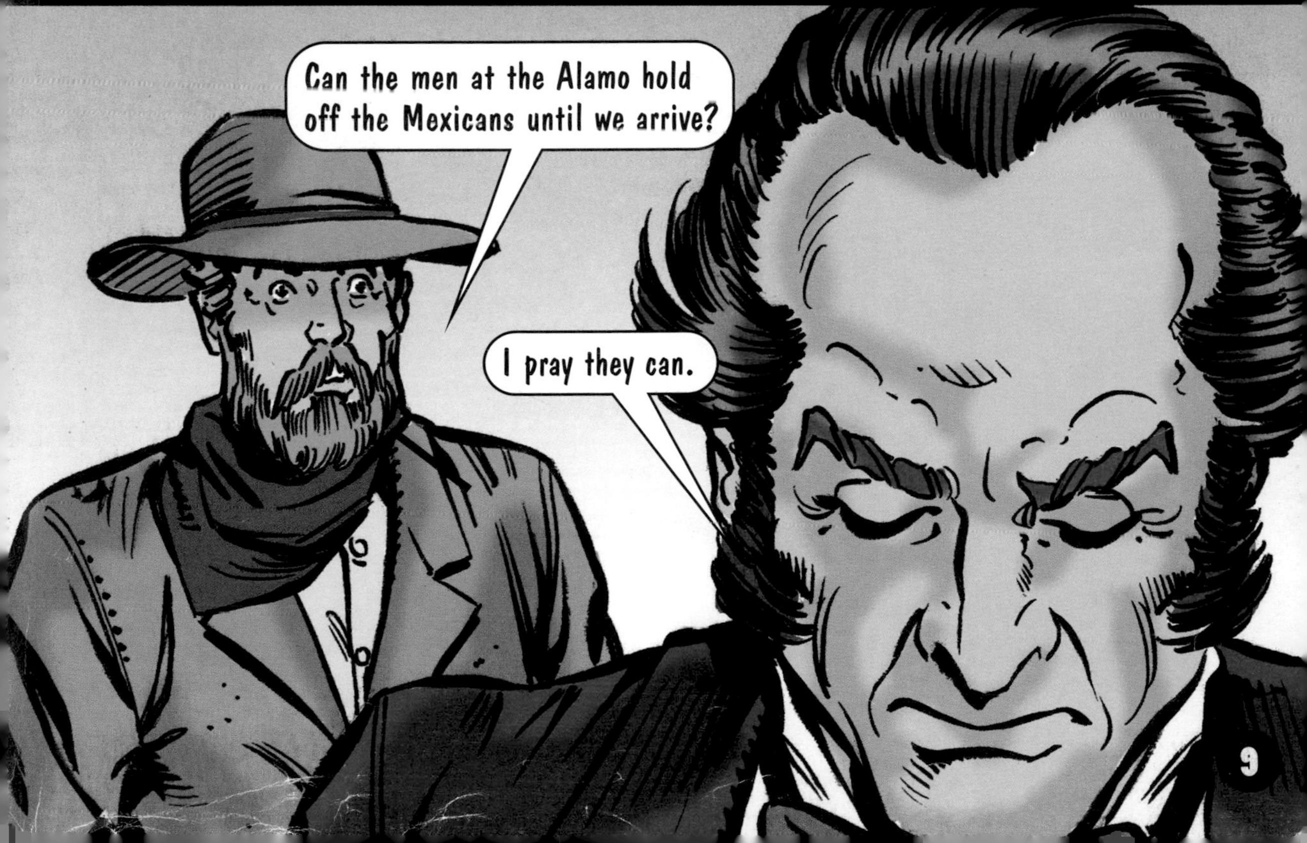
Can the men at the Alamo hold off the Mexicans until we arrive?
I pray they can.

CHAPTER 2

THE SIEGE

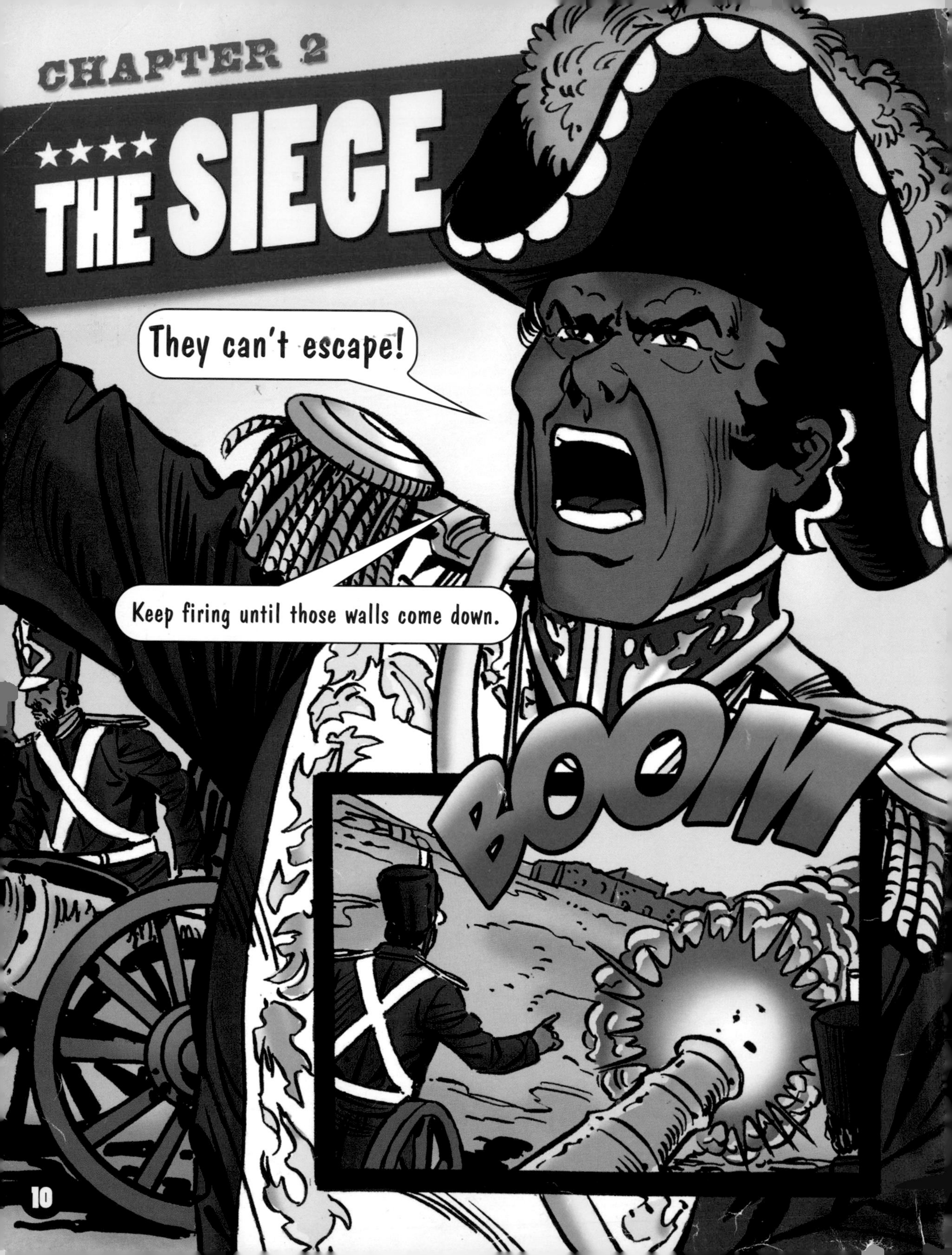
They can't escape!
Keep firing until those walls come down.
BOOM

Santa Anna and his armies had spread out around the Alamo. During this siege, they fired cannonball after cannonball at the walls. Each blast weakened the Alamo's outer defenses.
They fire all day, we patch all night. When are we supposed to sleep?
Never. I suppose that is the point.
Come on, boys. Just have to hold 'em off long enough for more Texan fighters to arrive.

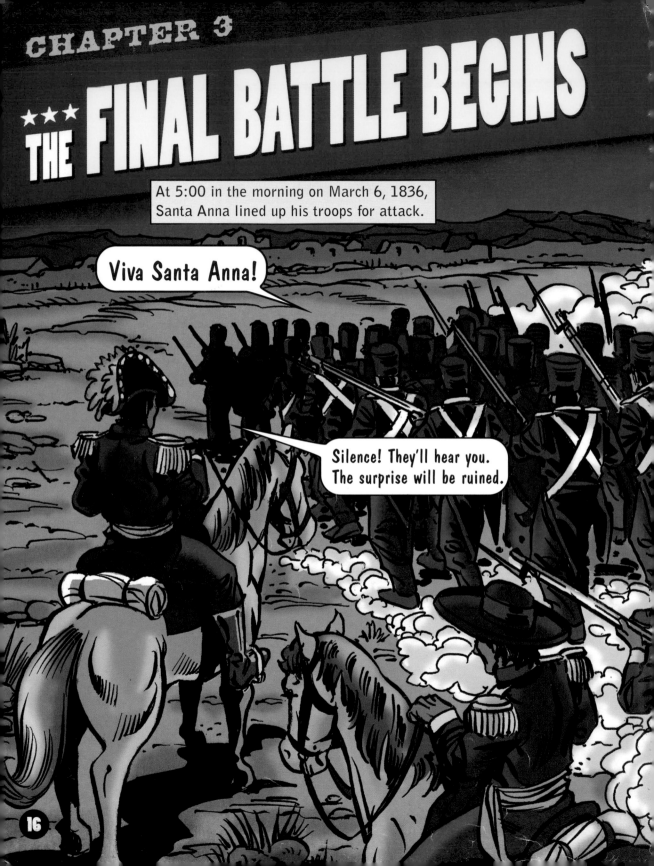

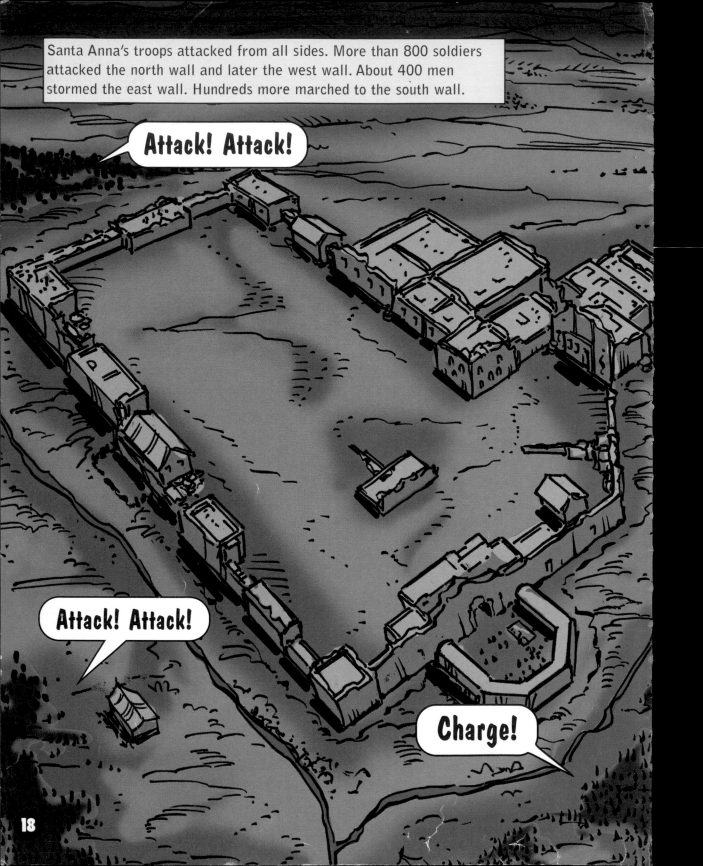

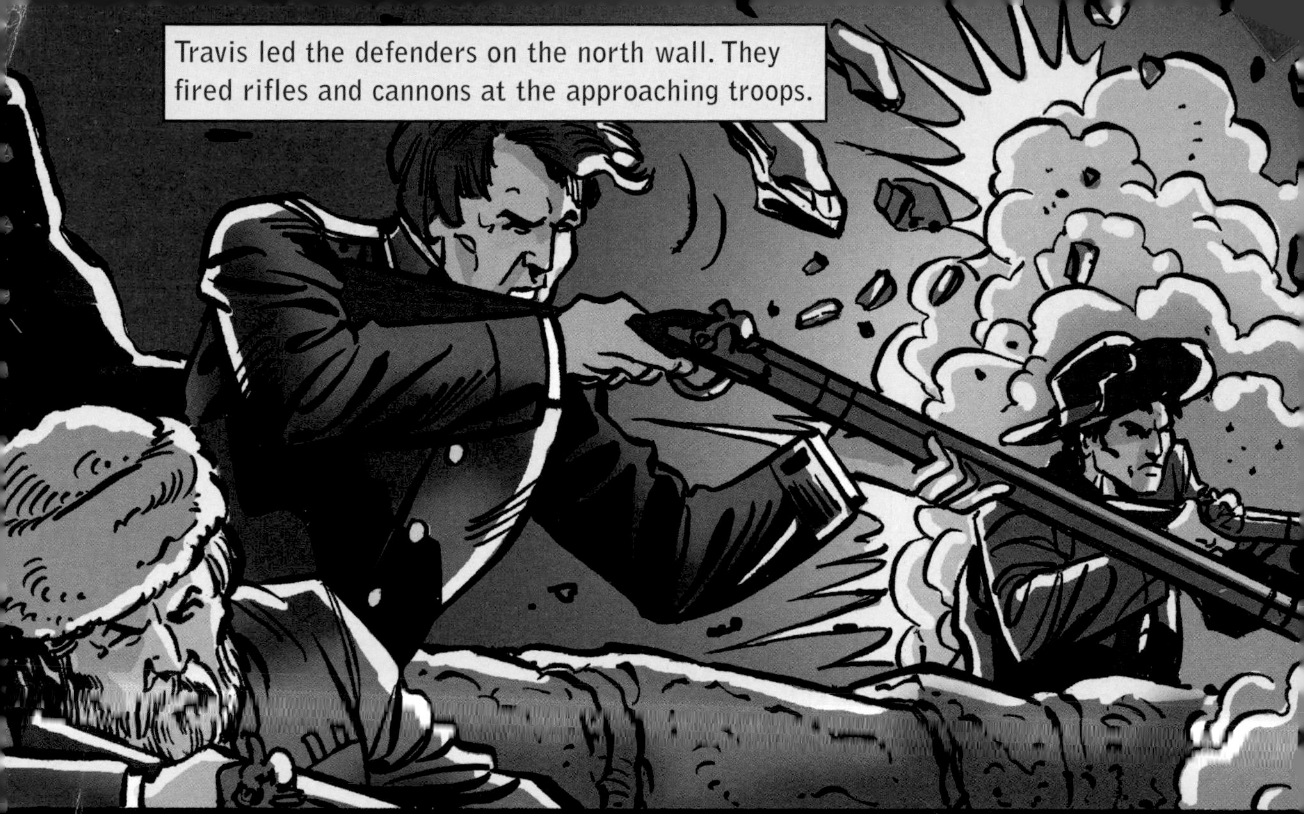
Travis led the defenders on the north wall. They fired rifles and cannons at the approaching troops.

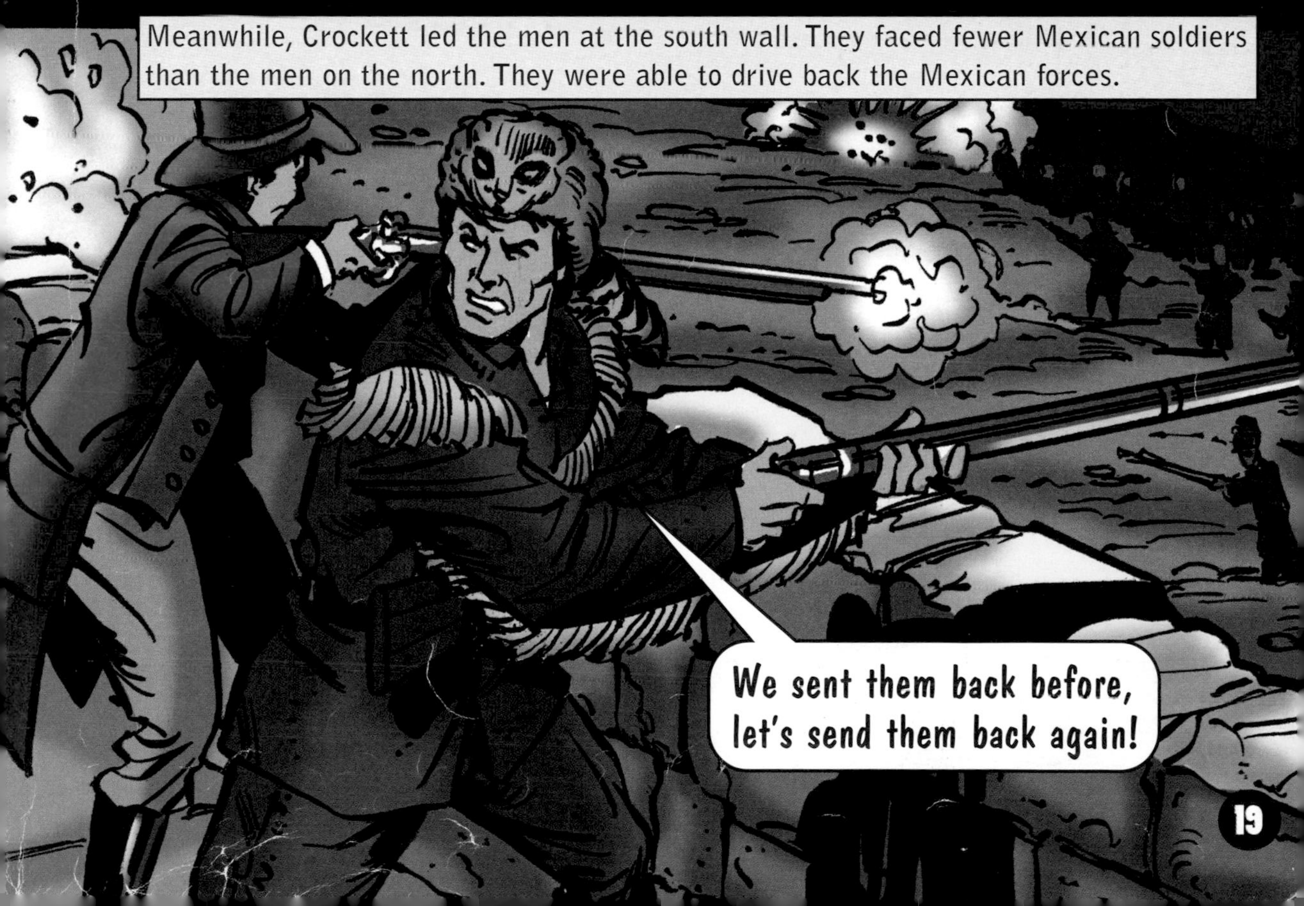
Meanwhile, Crockett led the men at the south wall. They faced fewer Mexican soldiers than the men on the north. They were able to drive back the Mexican forces.
We sent them back before, let's send them back again!

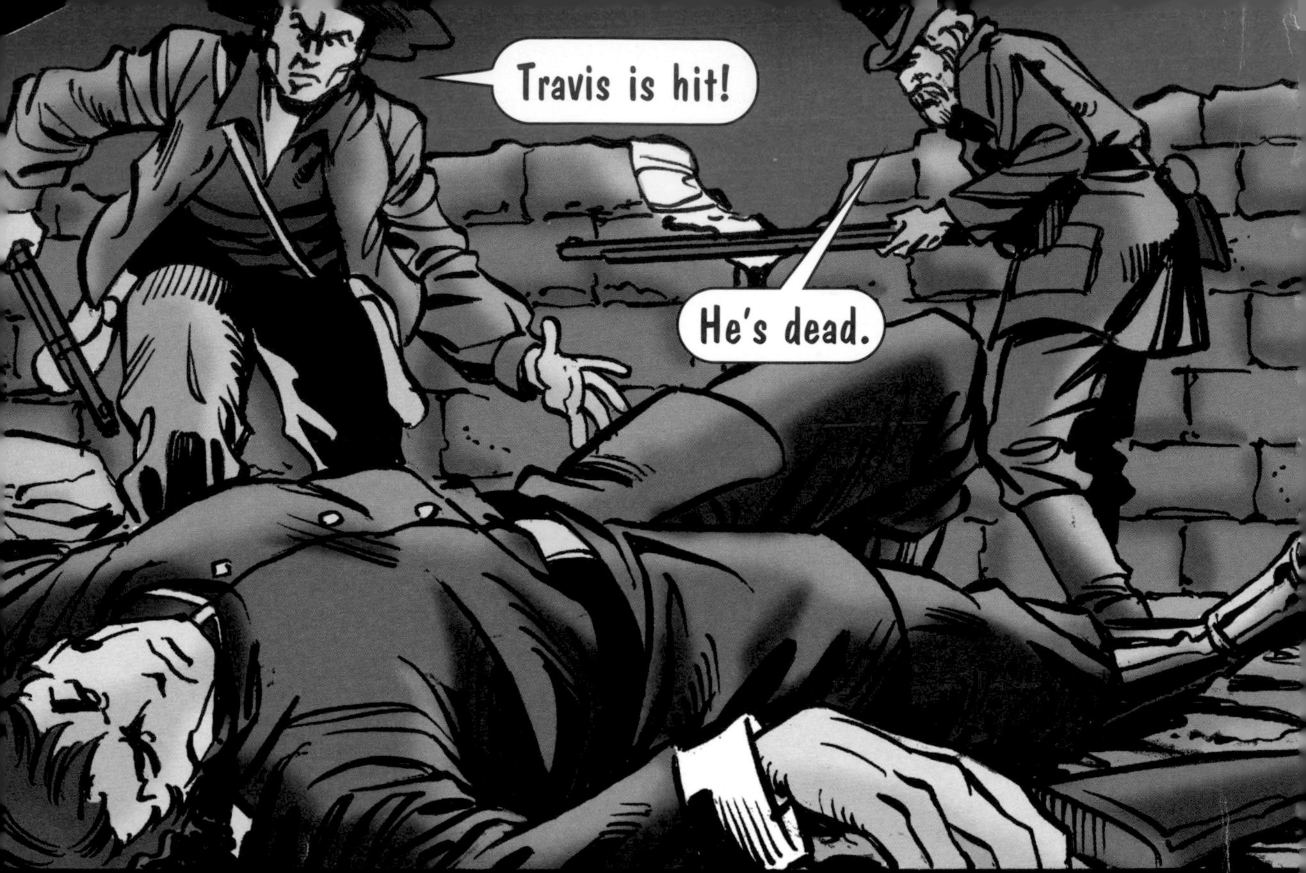
Travis is hit!
He's dead.

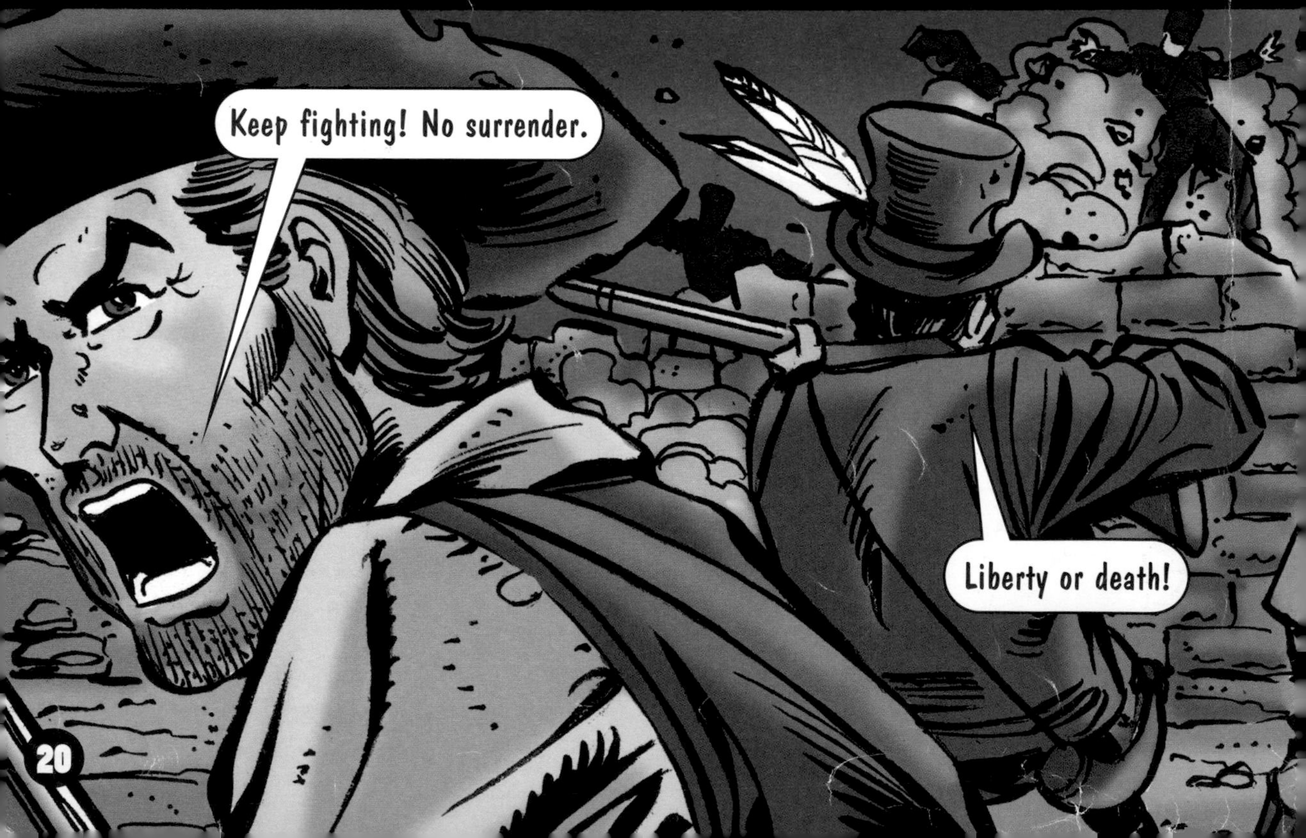
Keep fighting! No surrender.
Liberty or death!

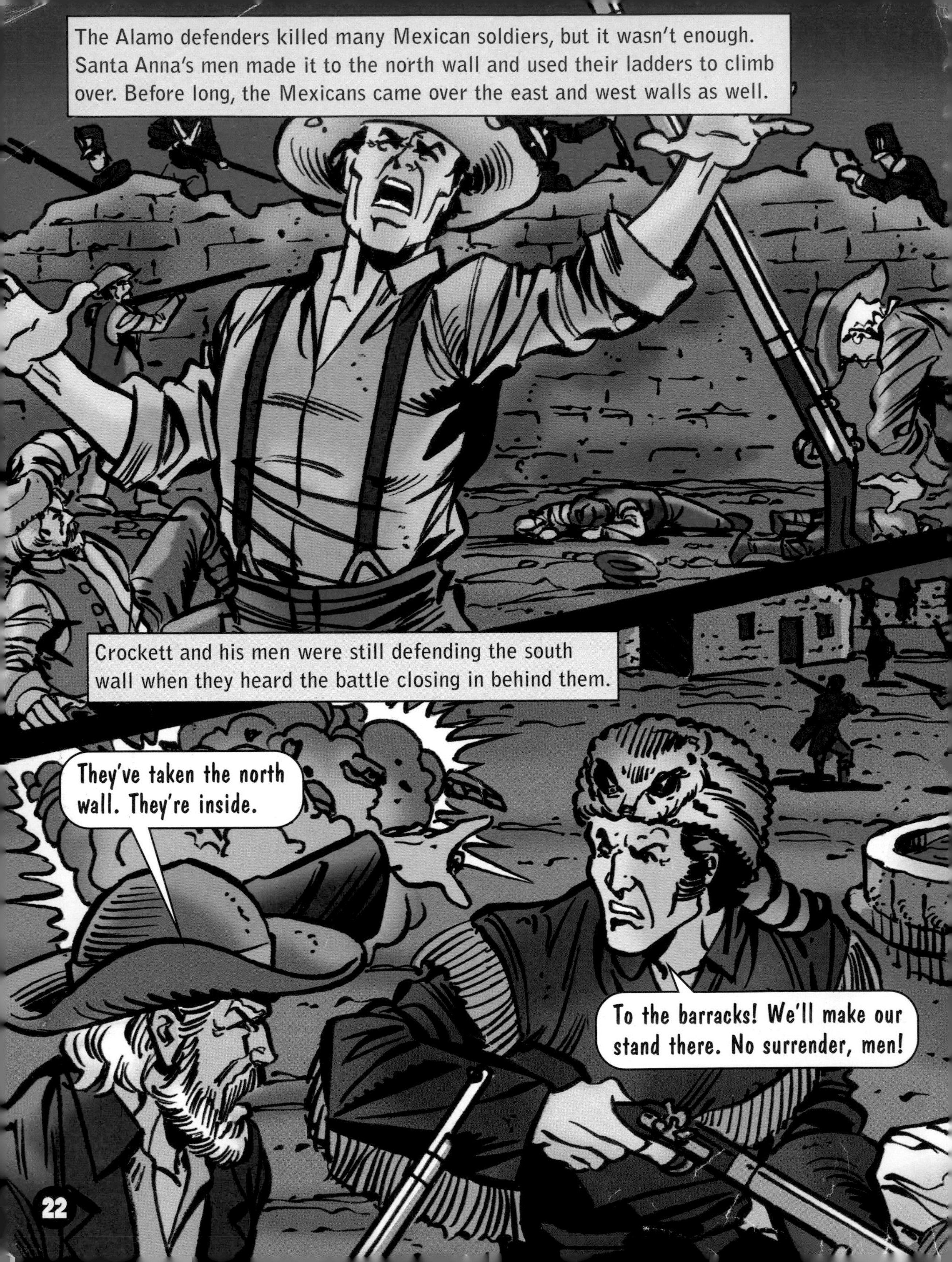
The Alamo defenders killed many Mexican soldiers, but it wasn't enough. Santa Anna's men made it to the north wall and used their ladders to climb over. Before long, the Mexicans came over the east and west walls as well.
Crockett and his men were still defending the south wall when they heard the battle closing in behind them.
They've taken the north wall. They're inside.
To the barracks! We'll make our stand there. No surrender, men!

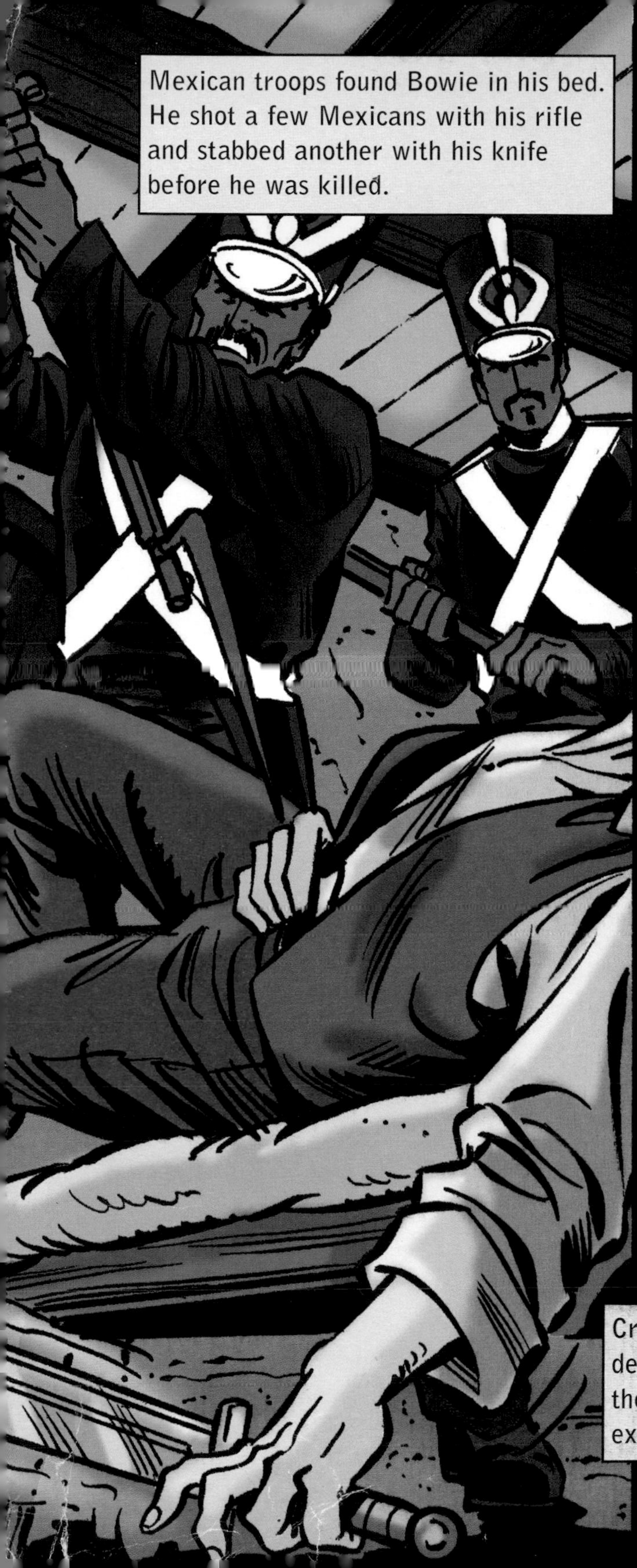
Mexican troops found Bowie in his bed. He shot a few Mexicans with his rifle and stabbed another with his knife before he was killed.

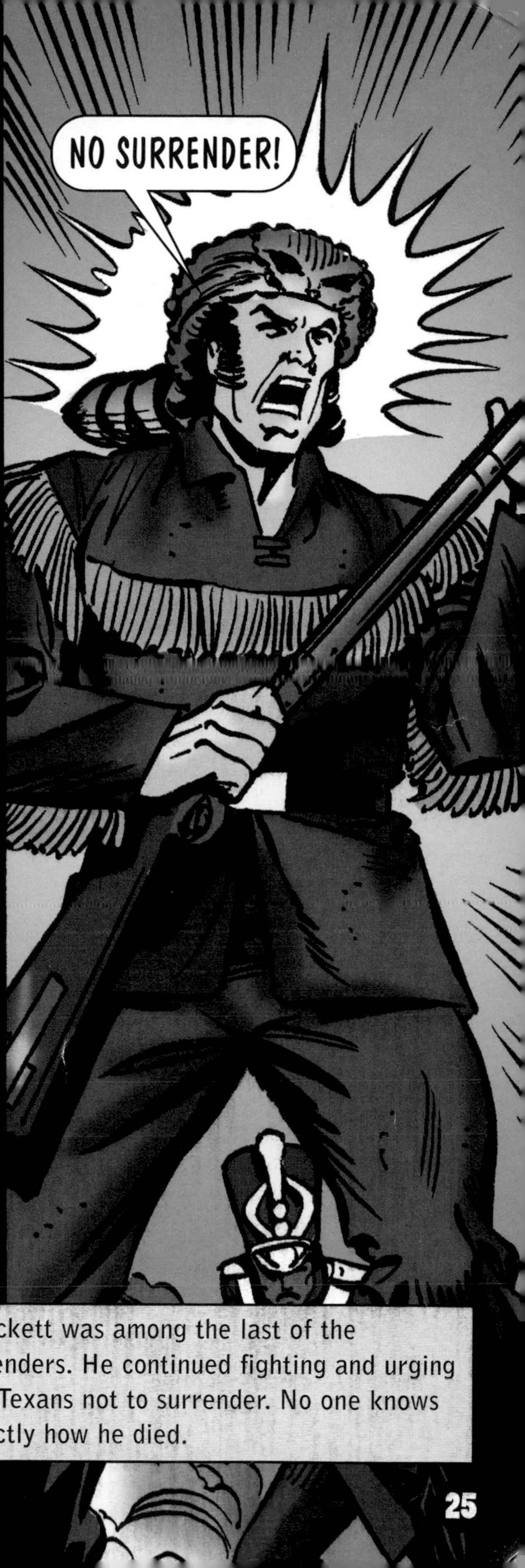
NO SURRENDER!
Crockett was among the last of the defenders. He continued fighting and urging the Texans not to surrender. No one knows exactly how he died.

Santa Anna showed no mercy. A few women and children were allowed to leave. One slave escaped. By sunrise, all the other defenders were dead.
Fire! Leave no man standing.
Burn the Texan bodies. Let everyone see how Mexico treats rebels!
Santa Anna's victory did not last long. His treatment of the Alamo defenders made the people of Texas fight harder for independence.

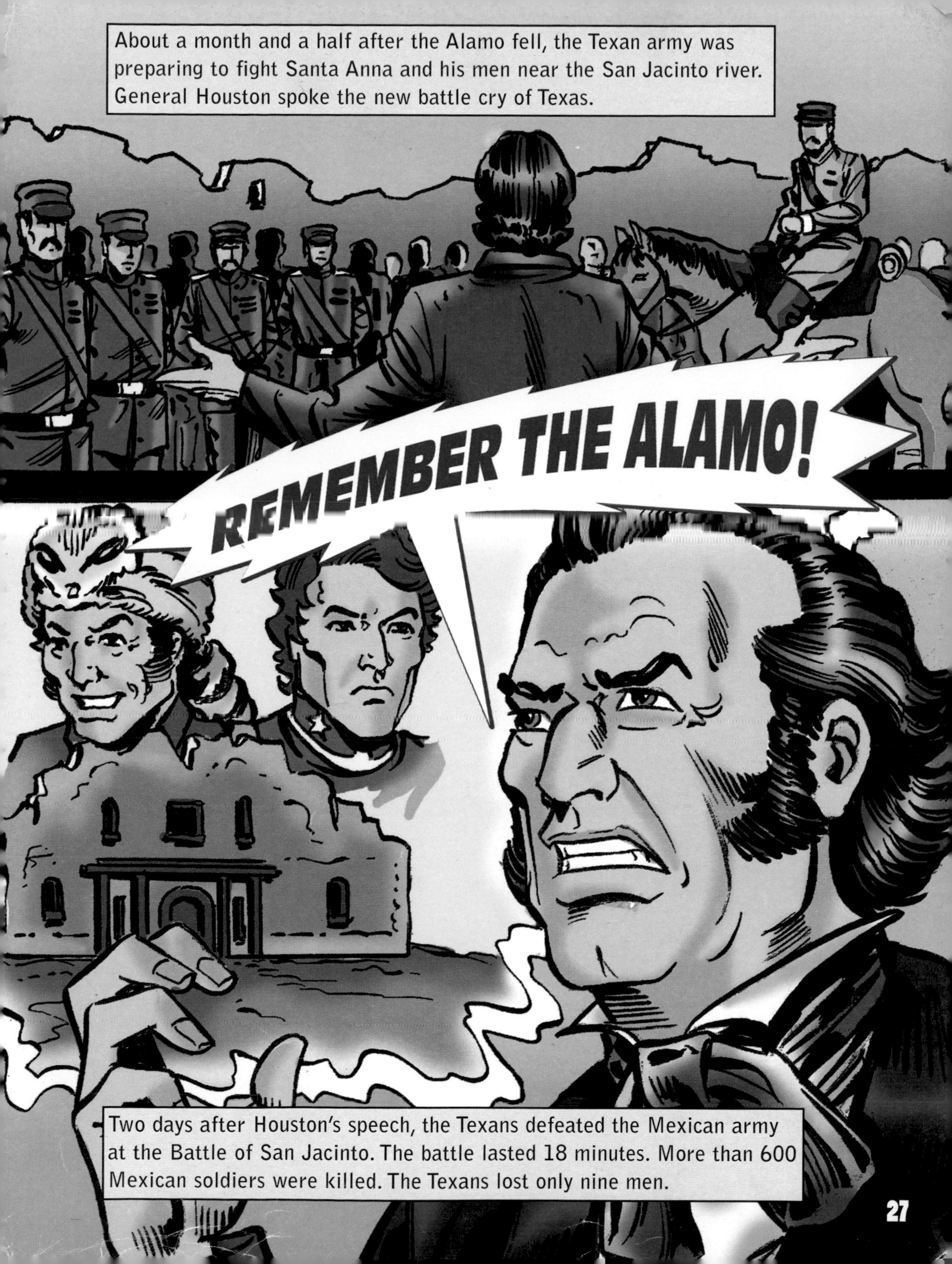
About a month and a half after the Alamo fell, the Texan army was preparing to fight Santa Anna and his men near the San Jacinto river. General Houston spoke the new battle cry of Texas.
REMEMBER THE ALAMO!
Two days after Houston's speech, the Texans defeated the Mexican army at the Battle of San Jacinto. The battle lasted 18 minutes. More than 600 Mexican soldiers were killed. The Texans lost only nine men.

MORE ABOUT ★★★ THE ALAMO

★ No one knows exactly how many people died in the Battle of the Alamo. Santa Anna reported that 600 men defended the Alamo, but most people think that the number was actually fewer than 200. Some people think that 500 or more Mexican soldiers died, but others say the number was much lower.

★ Not all of the Alamo defenders were Anglos. Some of Alamo's defenders were Tejanos. Tejanos were Hispanics who had settled in Texas.

★ Many of the Alamo defenders were not professional soldiers. They were volunteers who chose to help defend Texas. These men signed a contract when they volunteered. The contract kept them from quitting or leaving.

★ Santa Anna escaped from the Battle of San Jacinto dressed as a soldier instead of a general. He was captured the next day.

★ The Alamo was built in 1718 as a mission for American Indians who had converted to Christianity. More than 80 years later, it became a military fort.

★ Davy Crockett played the fiddle. Legend says he played his fiddle at the Alamo to cheer the men before battle. Today, the Witte Museum in San Antonio has one of Crockett's fiddles on display.

★ Jim Bowie was a frontiersman from Louisiana. He was famous for the large knife he carried and used in battles. Bowie knives are named for him.

★ William Travis was only 26 years old when he died defending the Alamo.

★ Texas gained its independence shortly after the Battle of the Alamo. It became its own country, with Sam Houston as president. In 1845, Texas became the 28th state in the United States.

GLOSSARY

Anglo (ANG-lo)—a white settler from a U.S. state or territory

barracks (BA-ruhks)—the part of a fort where soldiers sleep

fort (FORT)—a building that is well defended against attacks

legend (LEJ-uhnd)—a story handed down from earlier times

ruthless (ROOTH-liss)—cruel and unconcerned about others

siege (SEEJ)—an attack designed to surround a place and cut it off from supplies or help

surrender (suh-REN-dur)—to give up or admit defeat

volunteer (vol-uhn-TIHR)—someone who is not a professional soldier but offers to fight with an army; Colonel Jim Bowie led the volunteers assigned to the Alamo until he got sick; Crockett and his 12 men were volunteers from Tennessee.

INTERNET SITES

FactHound offers a safe, fun way to find Internet sites related to this book. All of the sites on FactHound have been researched by our staff.

Here's how:

1. Visit *www.facthound.com*
2. Type in this special code **0736838325** for age-appropriate sites. Or enter a search word related to this book for a more general search.
3. Click on the **Fetch It** button.

FactHound will fetch the best sites for you!

READ MORE

Bankston, John. *Antonio López de Santa Anna.* Latinos in American History. Bear, Del.: Mitchell Lane Publishers, 2004.

Burgan, Michael. *The Alamo.* We the People. Minneapolis: Compass Point Books, 2001.

Gaines, Ann. *The Alamo: The Fight over Texas.* Proud Heritage. Chanhassen, Minn.: Child's World, 2003.

Winders, Richard Bruce. *Davy Crockett.* The Legend of the Wild Frontier. New York: Power Plus Books, 2003.

BIBLIOGRAPHY

The Alamo in San Antonio, Texas. http://www.thealamo.org.

Daughters of the Republic of Texas Library. http://www.drtl.org.

Davis, William C. *Three Roads to the Alamo: The Lives and Fortunes of David Crockett, James Bowie, and William Barret Travis.* New York: HarperCollins, 1998.

Hardin, Stephen L. *Texan Iliad.* Austin, TX: University of Texas Press, 1994.

Long, Jeff. *Duel of Eagles: the Mexican and U.S. Fight for the Alamo.* New York: Morrow, 1990.

Murphy, Jim. *Inside the Alamo.* New York: Delacorte Press, 2003.

Texas A&M Digital Library. http://dl.tamu.edu/projects.html.

Texas State Library and Archives Commission. http://www.tsl.state.tx.us/treasures/republic/alamo-01.html.

INDEX